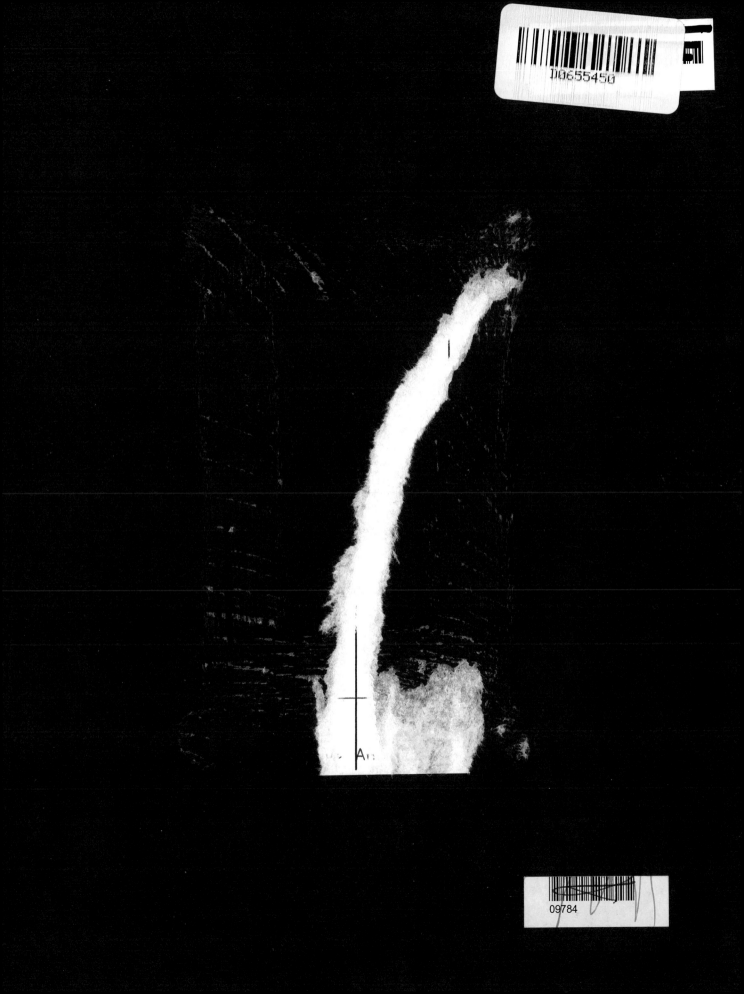

A SOLDIER'S LIFE IN

ANCIENT GREECE

A SOLDIER'S LIFE IN
ANCIENT GREECE

Fiona Corbridge

FRANKLIN WATTS
LONDON • SYDNEY

 Illustrations by
Mark Bergin
Giovanni Caselli
Chris Molan
Lee Montgomery
Peter Visscher
Maps by Stefan Chabluk

First published in 2006 by
Franklin Watts
338 Euston Road
London NW1 3BH

Franklin Watts Australia
Hachette Children's Books
Level 17/207 Kent Street
Sydney NSW 2000

Series editor: John C. Miles
Art director: Jonathan Hair

This book is based on
Going to War in Ancient Greece
by Adrian Gilbert © Franklin Watts 2000
It is produced for Franklin Watts
by Painted Fish Ltd.
Designer: Rita Storey

A CIP catalogue record
for this book is available
from the British Library

ISBN 0 7496 6492 4

Dewey classification: 355.00938

Printed in China

CONTENTS

Map: ANCIENT GREECE

MACEDONIA

Mt. Olympus

AEGEAN SEA

THESSALY

Thermopylae

BOEOTIA

Chaeronea

Leuctra

Plataea

Corinth

Salamis

Argos

PELOPONNESE

MESSENIA • Sparta

LACONIA

Athens

Thebes

Marathon

Piraeus

PAROS

ANCIENT GREECE

Greek settlements
(places where Greeks lived)

Land battles

Sea battles

• **Greek cities**

Massilia

Neapolis

ADRIATIC SEA

Syracuse

Kinyps

TRIPOLIS

THE ANCIENT GREEKS

The people who we call the ancient Greeks lived from around 750 to 338 BCE. Greece was made up of many city-states. Some of these were small towns and the land around them. Other city-states, such as Athens and Sparta, were bigger and more powerful. Each city-state had an army, and they often fought each other.

Armour found in the city of Argos. It is from the eighth century BCE

Mycenaeans
1200 BCE
A people called the Mycenaeans lived in Greece until 1200 BCE.

City-states
750–650 BCE
City-states begin to grow up in Greece.

Persian invasions
490–479 BCE
The Persians try to invade Greece twice, but the Greeks fight them off.

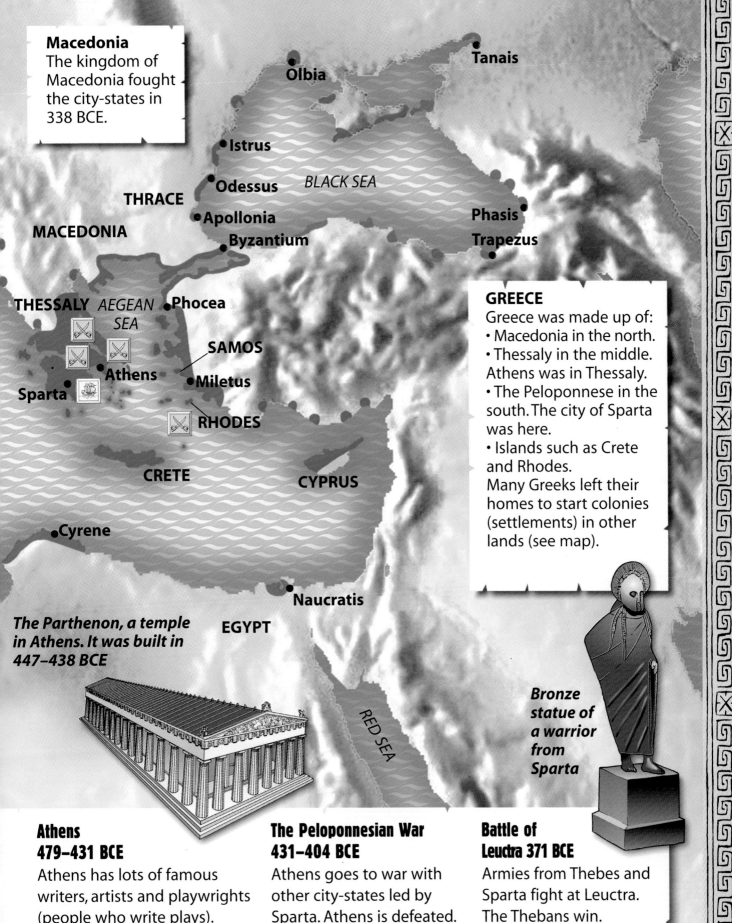

Macedonia
The kingdom of Macedonia fought the city-states in 338 BCE.

Tanais

Olbia

Istrus

Odessus

BLACK SEA

THRACE

Apollonia

MACEDONIA

Byzantium

Phasis

Trapezus

THESSALY

AEGEAN
SEA

Phocea

SAMOS

Athens

Miletus

Sparta

RHODES

CRETE

CYPRUS

Cyrene

Naucratis

EGYPT

RED SEA

GREECE
Greece was made up of:
• Macedonia in the north.
• Thessaly in the middle. Athens was in Thessaly.
• The Peloponnese in the south. The city of Sparta was here.
• Islands such as Crete and Rhodes.
Many Greeks left their homes to start colonies (settlements) in other lands (see map).

The Parthenon, a temple in Athens. It was built in 447–438 BCE

Bronze statue of a warrior from Sparta

Athens
479–431 BCE
Athens has lots of famous writers, artists and playwrights (people who write plays).

The Peloponnesian War
431–404 BCE
Athens goes to war with other city-states led by Sparta. Athens is defeated.

Battle of
Leuctra 371 BCE
Armies from Thebes and Sparta fight at Leuctra. The Thebans win.

JOINING THE ARMY

Each city-state had soldiers called *hoplites*. Hoplites were infantry soldiers (soldiers who fought on foot).

Athens was the largest city-state and it had a huge army. Ten generals were in charge of it. When Athens was not at war, the generals helped to run the government.

FARMERS

Most hoplites were farmers. They worked as soldiers as well as running their farms. They had enough money to buy the weapons and armour they needed.

Wars happened quickly, so the farmers were not away from their farms for long.

Hoplites getting ready for war

ATHENS AT WAR

When there was a war, all citizens over seventeen had to join the army and fight. Only men could be citizens. Women and slaves were not allowed to be. Citizens could vote.

FAMOUS ARMY COMMANDERS

Militiades
(550–489 BCE)
Militiades defeated the Persians at the battle of Marathon (490 BCE).

Pericles
(495–429 BCE)
Pericles (below) helped Athens to become more powerful in the fifth century BCE.

PEPIKΛHΣ

Alexander the Great
(356–323 BCE)
Alexander came from Macedonia. His father had defeated the city-states so Alexander's army was made up of Greeks and Macedonians. Alexander took over many lands to make a huge empire.

FIGHTING IN THE ARMY
The Greeks thought it was a great thing to fight in the army. All sorts of people did it. The playwright Sophocles (496–406 BCE) was a commander in the navy. The author Aeschylus (525–456 BCE) fought the Persians at Marathon.

DEATH SENTENCE
After the sea battle of Arginusae in 406 BCE, eight commanders from Athens were sentenced to death because they had not rescued Athenian sailors who fell in the water. Socrates tried to stop them being killed, but he did not succeed.

Socrates the philosopher (469–399 BCE) fought as a hoplite

SPARTANS

The Spartans were a Greek people who lived in the city-state of Sparta in the Peloponnese.

Spartan citizens (men born in Sparta) had to join the army. They were not allowed to do any other work, and spent all their time training for war.

Life in Sparta
The Spartans lived in hard conditions. People were not rich and were not allowed to own gold or silver. Luxuries (things that are nice to have but not really necessary) were banned.

UNIFORM

Spartan soldiers wore red tunics (like a dress) and cloaks, which made them stand out on the battlefield. They had long hair, which they combed carefully before a battle.

SPARTAN SOLDIERS

Spartan soldiers were very brave and had great fighting skills.

All soldiers had to live in buildings called barracks. They were not allowed to marry until they were thirty years old, and were only allowed to visit their family occasionally.

A Spartan soldier

Stone statue of King Leonidas of Sparta

THE PERSIAN INVASION

In 480 BCE, a huge Persian army invaded Greece. King Leonidas and his small Spartan army held them up at Thermopylae. The Spartans fought bravely, but were all killed.

FIGHTING THE PERSIANS

Because Leonidas and his men were so brave, the other Greek city-states fought against the Persians too.

The Persians marched south and captured Athens. Then they were defeated in the sea battle of Salamis.

The next year, the Persians were beaten on land at the battle of Plataea and chased out of Greece.

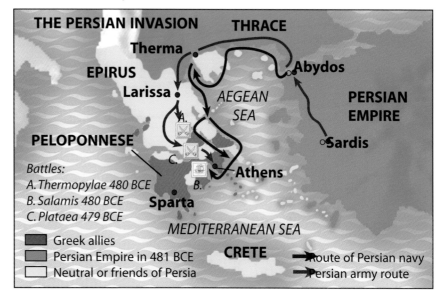

THE PERSIAN INVASION

THRACE

Therma

Abydos

EPIRUS

Larissa

AEGEAN SEA

PERSIAN EMPIRE

PELOPONNESE

A.

Sardis

Battles:
A. Thermopylae 480 BCE
B. Salamis 480 BCE
C. Plataea 479 BCE

C.

B.

Athens

Sparta

MEDITERRANEAN SEA

Greek allies
Persian Empire in 481 BCE
Neutral or friends of Persia

CRETE

Route of Persian navy
Persian army route

HARD LIVES

Spartan boys

At the age of seven, boys were sent away to school. Rules and exercise were important. The boys had a hard life to get them ready for being soldiers.

Spartan girls

Spartan girls did lots of sport. This was to make them fit and strong so that when they became mothers, they would have healthy children.

Helots

Helots were people captured by the Spartans. They worked as slaves, farming the land. The Spartans were always worried that the helots would rebel (fight them).

HOPLITES

When there was a battle, hoplites lined up in a shape called a formation. They stood very close together to fight. This formation was called a *phalanx*. It was a very good way of fighting.

🛡️ BODY ARMOUR

Hoplites wore body armour called a cuirass. It was made out of a material called linen, which had been stiffened. Sometimes cuirasses were made out of leather or bronze.

They also wore a bronze helmet to protect the head.

🛡️ LEG ARMOUR

On their legs, hoplites wore greaves. These were made of thin bronze and clipped around their calves.

The hoplites could fix a leather apron to the shield to give their legs extra protection.

Bronze helmet

Horsehair plume

Linen tunic

Stiffened linen cuirass

Sword

Argive shield

Leather apron

Bronze greaves

Spear

Sandals

Butt spike

WEAPONS

Swords

Hoplites only used their short iron swords if their spears were broken, or for close-up fighting.

Spear

Shield

Sword

Shields

The round, curved shield used by the hoplites was called an argive shield. It was a symbol of courage and was often decorated.

Spears

The hoplites' main weapon was a spear. A spear was a sharp, pointed metal blade on a long stick. It could be thrown at enemies, or used to stab them.

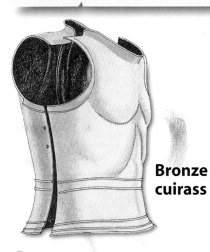

Bronze cuirass

🛡 CUIRASS

The cuirass protected the chest and back. Heavy bronze cuirasses were sometimes shaped to show the muscles of the body. They were made of two plates joined at the sides.

Corinthian helmet

🛡 A HEAVY WEIGHT

The hoplites' armour and weapons were very heavy. They weighed about half as much as a man. Because of this, hoplites could not move very fast.

Back of a hoplite's shield showing holding straps

🛡 CORINTHIAN HELMET

This heavy helmet covered a lot of the face. It was very popular in the fifth and sixth centuries BCE.

It had a plume on top which both looked good and helped hoplites to recognize each other in a battle.

CAVALRY AND SKIRMISHERS

During the fifth century BCE, the Greeks began to use different kinds of soldiers, such as cavalry (troops on horseback). The phalanx of hoplites was good at fighting on flat, open ground. But the army also started to use soldiers called skirmishers in hills and on rough land. Skirmishers attacked the enemy's phalanx before the main battle.

Tactics
Tactics are special plans that an army makes to try and win in battle.

A commander called Iphicrates thought that the best tactic was to use cavalrymen and other troops next to a phalanx.

THE CAVALRY
Cavalrymen usually came from wealthy families, because it was expensive to keep horses.

The best cavalrymen came from the state of Thessaly. Men from there were very good riders.

CAVALRY IN ACTION
A cavalryman rode his horse without stirrups and a saddle. He did not usually wear armour, and carried two javelins and a sword. In a battle, he threw the javelins at enemy soldiers and then rode back to safety. He was not expected to do close-up fighting.

Cavalryman

OTHER TROOPS

Different soldiers helped the phalanxes. *Psiloi* and *gymnets* were skirmishers. *Peltasts* came from Thrace. There were also archers and slingers.

PSILOI
Used a club and threw stones at the enemy.

GYMNETS
Only had swords. Not much use in a big battle.

ARCHERS
Had powerful bows that fired arrows a long way.

SLINGERS
Fired stones at the enemy very accurately.

PELTASTS
Armed with javelins and a crescent-shaped shield.

SLINGSHOTS, BOWS AND ARROWS

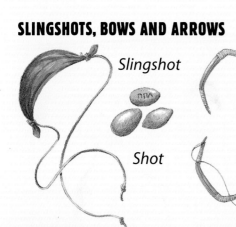

Slingshot

Shot

Strung bow

Unstrung bow

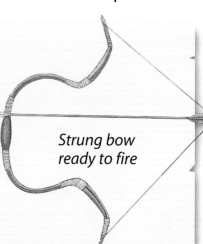

Strung bow ready to fire

Slingshots
Slingers used a leather slingshot to fire shot at the enemy. Shot was made from small stones, clay or lead. It could kill.

Composite bows
Composite bows were made of wood, horn, bone and animal sinews. They could fire arrows a long way to hit a target.

Drawing the bow
The most powerful composite bows were very difficult to draw back, so archers had to be extremely strong.

FIGHTING IN A PHALANX

The hoplites began to fight in phalanxes (close formations) in about 750 BCE.

A flat piece of land was chosen for the battleground. The two armies lined up, facing each other. When the order to attack was given, the two sides rushed towards each other and fierce fighting began.

BOEOTIA
Thebes
Leuctra •
Battle of Leuctra 371 BCE
•Athens
PELOPONNESE
MESSENIA
•Sparta
LACONIA *MEDITERRANEAN SEA*

🏛 BATTLE OF LEUCTRA

In 371 BCE, the Theban army used the phalanx in a new way. It helped them to defeat the more powerful Spartan army (see below).

BATTLES

Phalanx at work

A phalanx could be several hundred men across and from eight to sixteen men deep. The first three rows stabbed at the enemy with spears. Those behind tried to push them forward to break the enemy line.

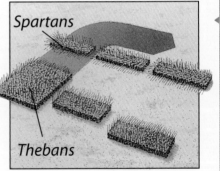

Spartans

Thebans

Wall of shields

Because the men of the phalanx stood close together, their shields formed a protective wall.

Clever Thebans

At Leuctra, Thebans used one phalanx that was fifty men deep, and two smaller ones. The Spartan phalanxes were only twelve men deep. The big Theban phalanx attacked first and mowed down the Spartans.

CLASH OF SHIELDS

Hoplites had to be very brave and strong. Once the two sides were fighting, the side that pushed forward and broke into the enemy's phalanx won the battle. Each hoplite used his shield for protection and tried to stab the enemy. A battle was terrifying. Anyone who fell was trampled.

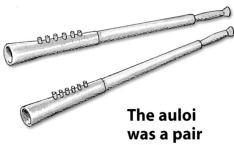

The auloi was a pair of pipes

MARCHING TO MUSIC

Musicians playing horns and *aulois* went into battle too. The music helped the hoplites keep in step as they marched. This was important so that the phalanx stayed close together.

Musician playing the auloi

Attackers and defenders

• *A phalanx was a formation of hoplites fighting close together.*

• *The first few rows of a phalanx were the attackers. They fought the enemy with their weapons.*

• *The rest of the phalanx were defenders. They linked their shields to make a wall that protected them. It also helped stop the enemy breaking through.*

SIEGE WARFARE

A siege was an attack on a walled city (a city with protective walls around it) or a fortress. Soldiers surrounded it and stopped the people getting any food or supplies. The army attacked the city or fortress with special weapons, and used towers and ladders.

The Greeks did not use sieges until the Peloponnesian War in 431–404 BCE.

SIEGE IN PROGRESS

The attacking army had lots of ways of trying to take over the city. They tunnelled under the walls to try and make them fall down. They used battering rams to smash their way through.

They fired crossbows and catapults. Siege towers were pushed into place so that the army could get over the walls.

Siege tower

Battering ram

SUCCESSFUL SIEGES

Dionysius I of Syracuse (in Sicily) used the latest siege equipment, such as catapults and towers, to attack Moyta in 397 BCE.

In Macedonia, King Philip II and his son Alexander the Great copied these ideas and became very good at siege warfare.

SIEGE WEAPONS

Catapult

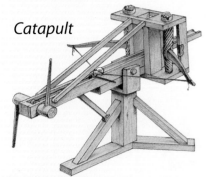
Catapult

Large crossbow

A large siege crossbow was fired from a stand. The string to fire the arrow was pulled back with a handle called a winch. Then the handle was released so the arrow shot out.

Catapult

The catapult had an arm at either side to fire stones. Each arm was held in place by tightly twisted sinew or horsehair. This provided the power to fire the stone.

Battering ram

Battering ram

This was a tree trunk with a metal point on the end. It hung from a frame. Soldiers swung the ram against the city walls to smash through weak points. The roof and sides were covered in leather to stop the soldiers being hit by arrows.

Crossbow

🏛 PELOPONNESIAN WAR

This war lasted for twenty-five years (431–404 BCE). On one side was a group of city-states led by Sparta. On the other side was Athens and its supporters. Eventually, the Spartans won.

🏛 SIEGE TOWERS

A siege tower was an armoured tower on wheels. Soldiers fought from it and used it to get over city walls.

This tower was made for the siege of Rhodes in 305–304 BCE. It was called the city-taker.

42 metres high

Iron plates   *Catapult*

The city-taker (*helepolis*)

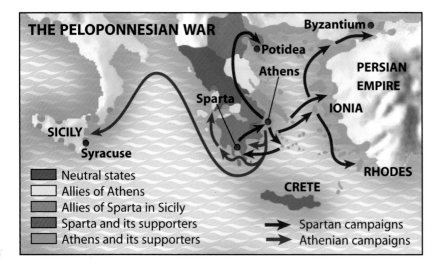

THE PELOPONNESIAN WAR

Byzantium

Potidea

Athens

PERSIAN
EMPIRE

Sparta

IONIA

SICILY

Syracuse

RHODES

CRETE

Neutral states
Allies of Athens
Allies of Sparta in Sicily
Sparta and its supporters
Athens and its supporters

→ Spartan campaigns
→ Athenian campaigns

WAR AT SEA

The Greeks built their ships like those of the Phoenicians, a seafaring people who lived around the Mediterranean. In the eighth century BCE, the Greeks had a ship called a *bireme*, which had two rows of oars. In the fifth century BCE, they built the *trireme,* which had three rows of oars.

ATHENS AND THE SEA

The city-state of Athens had a powerful navy. This helped it to win fights and create a large empire.

The navy needed lots of men to row its ships. Once, it used over 20,000 men. Men who could not afford to buy the armour and weapons needed to be a hoplite became rowers instead.

A trireme

Large single sail

Banks of rowers

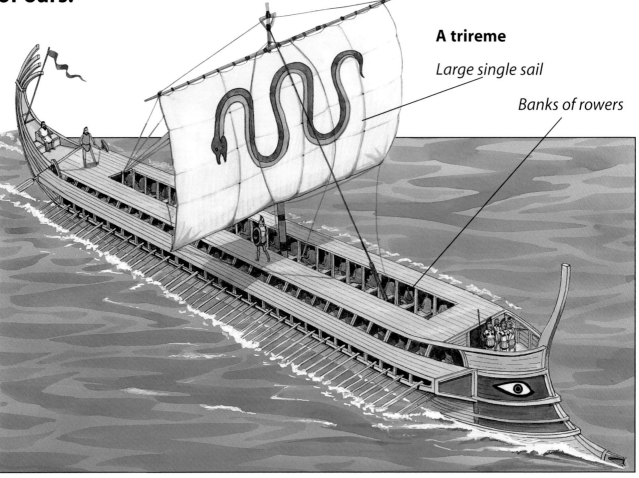

THE TRIREME

Triremes had 170 rowers and 30 crewmen and marines. When a trireme was at sea, it usually kept near the coast. In the evenings it sailed to the shore and the crew spent the night on land. Before battle, the sail was taken down. Rowers kept the ship moving.

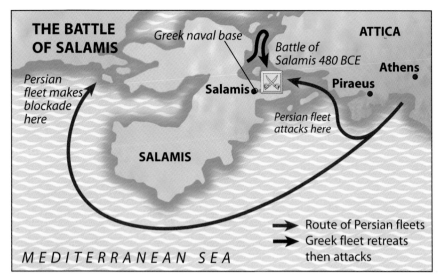

THE BATTLE OF SALAMIS

ATTICA

Greek naval base

Battle of Salamis 480 BCE

Athens

Piraeus

Salamis

Persian fleet makes blockade here

SALAMIS

Persian fleet attacks here

→ Route of Persian fleets
→ Greek fleet retreats then attacks

MEDITERRANEAN SEA

BATTLE OF SALAMIS

The second time the Persians tried to invade Greece, there was a sea battle around the island of Salamis. There were 200 Greek ships and 800 Persian ships. But the Greeks were so good at fighting and rowing that they defeated the Persians.

RAMMING SHIPS

The prow (front) of the trireme was made of bronze, for ramming enemy ships. The rowers made the trireme travel fast enough for the ram to put a hole in the side of an enemy's ship. They hoped this would sink it.

Painted eye to keep evil away

Bronze prow of trireme

BATTLE TACTICS

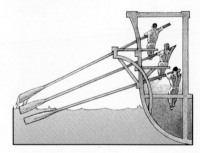

Sinking the enemy

An attacking ship sailed straight at an enemy ship to ram it in the side. The enemy ship could be so badly damaged that it would sink in a few minutes.

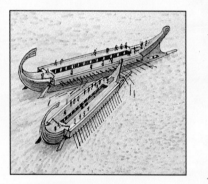

Rowing a trireme

There were three rows of oars, one above the other. The rowers could reach an amazing speed of 16 km/h for short periods of time.

Destroying oars

Sometimes a trireme went next to an enemy ship and smashed its oars. Now the enemy ship couldn't move, so the attackers could get on it or ram it.

AN ARMY ON THE MOVE

When an army went off to fight, servants and slaves carried the baggage. Mules, horses and carts moved heavy things.

On a march, hoplites usually ate barley porridge. Sometimes they had cheese, salted meat and onions. They would also help themselves to things growing nearby, such as figs and olives.

CLEARING THE WAY

The Spartan army used men to clear the path ahead so that the army's equipment could be moved to where it was needed. They used shovels, axes and sickles (tools with a curved blade).

Cavalryman

Packhorse

Servant

Foot soldier

CAMP FOLLOWERS

When an army was going off to fight for a long time, it took people to help repair arms and equipment. There were blacksmiths, carpenters and leather-workers.

The hoplites' families and servants went too. They were called camp followers. Sometimes there were so many camp followers that it slowed the army down.

BEFORE BATTLE

A hoplite got ready carefully before a battle. He combed his hair before putting on his helmet. Then he put on his cuirass, and fastened greaves on his legs. He got out his shield, which was a very special and important object to him.

Vase painting showing hoplites getting ready for battle

SLAVES AND SERVANTS

The Spartans used helots and the Athenians used farm workers or slaves to carry armour and weapons. These servants also got food ready, built shelters and cleaned weapons.

A servant packs a shield in its leather cover

WOUNDED SOLDIERS

The Greeks tried to help men who were injured in battle, but they did not know a lot about how the body worked. If a soldier's wounds became infected he would probably die. Some armies had surgeons.

Greek surgical instruments

WAR AND THE GODS

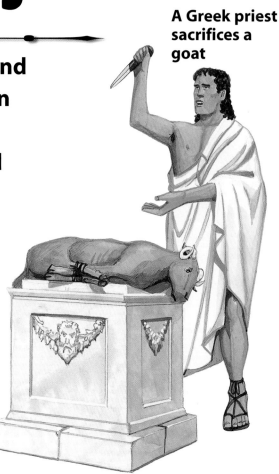

A Greek priest sacrifices a goat

The Greeks believed in many gods and goddesses. They worshipped them in buildings called temples.

Before battle, a commander would order the sacrifice (killing) of a goat or a sheep. He hoped that the sacrifice would please the gods and persuade them to help his army to win.

GODS

Athene

Athene was the goddess of wisdom and war. She was often shown wearing hoplite armour. Athens was named after her.

Ares

The god of war was called Ares. He was violent and bad-tempered.

Nike

Nike was a beautiful goddess with wings. She sometimes had a spear and shield. Her name meant "victory". There were many statues of her in Greece.

Home of the gods
The Greeks believed that the gods lived on top of Mount Olympus. The king of the gods was Zeus, who ruled the heavens. His brother Poseidon was in charge of the sea. Another brother, Hades, ruled the underworld, where people went when they died.

SOPHOCLES (c. 496–406 BCE)

The playwright Sophocles was also a naval commander. He wrote about his experiences of war in his plays.

A hoplite winning a battle

PRISONERS

To begin with, the city-states usually swapped their prisoners after a battle. But during the Peloponnesian War, (431–404 BCE) this started to change. Prisoners were often killed.

A Spartan hoplite gets ready to kill a prisoner

RULES OF WAR

The hoplites were meant to follow rules of war called the *nomima*. The rules said that hoplites should be brave in battle and behave well when they won. They had to treat prisoners fairly.

THE ARMY OF MACEDONIA

In 359 BCE, Philip II became king of the northern kingdom of Macedonia. He built up a strong army and began to attack Greek city-states. He wanted to get control of them.

Philip's army beat the city-states at the battle of Chaeronea in 338 BCE. Now Philip had Greece in his power.

Macedonian troops
• *The Macedonian phalanx was a formation of soldiers called phalangites.*

• *There were cavalrymen along the sides of the phalanx to help it.*

• *Peltasts were soldiers armed with javelins, who carried a crescent-shaped shield.*

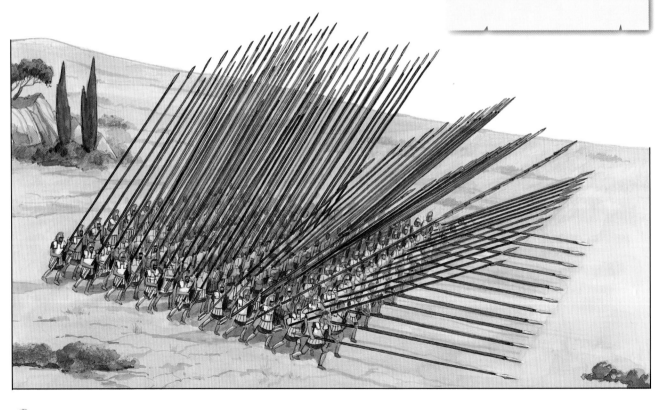

MACEDONIAN PHALANX

The hoplites in a Greek phalanx formed a wall to defend themselves. A Macedonian phalanx was more interested in attacking the enemy. Soldiers wore lightweight armour and carried a very long spear. The first five rows pointed their spears at the enemy.

PHILIP'S ARMY

Philip had a new type of infantry called *hypaspists*. They were armed with short spears and swords, and protected the phalanx.

Philip had followers from noble families, called Companions. Most of them fought on horseback. The cavalry was very important in the army.

A phalangite's spear was up to 6 m long

THE PHALANGITES

The soldiers of the Macedonian phalanx were called *phalangites*. The phalangites held a long spear in both hands. They had a small shield on a leather strap, which they wore over their shoulder. The soldiers were very well trained.

MACEDONIANS AT WAR

Carving of Philip II

Philip II

Philip (c. 382–336 BCE) was a clever general. He put different types of troops together to beat his enemies.

Macedonian helmets

The Macedonians wore the Thracian helmet. It did not cover the whole face, so the soldier could see and hear properly during a battle.

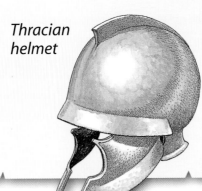

Thracian helmet

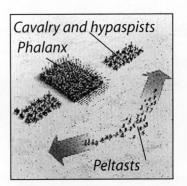

Cavalry and hypaspists
Phalanx
Peltasts

Fighting a battle

Peltasts started the attack. Then the main phalanx, cavalry and hypaspists took over. The peltasts went to the back.

ALEXANDER THE GREAT

Alexander the Great was the son of King Philip of Macedonia. He took over from Philip in 336 BCE. He immediately started to build a huge empire in the east. Eventually, Alexander controlled an empire that stretched throughout Asia and part of Africa.

THE COMPANIONS

These cavalrymen were the top troops of Alexander's army. They carried a long spear.

The Companions arranged themselves in formation to charge at the enemy.

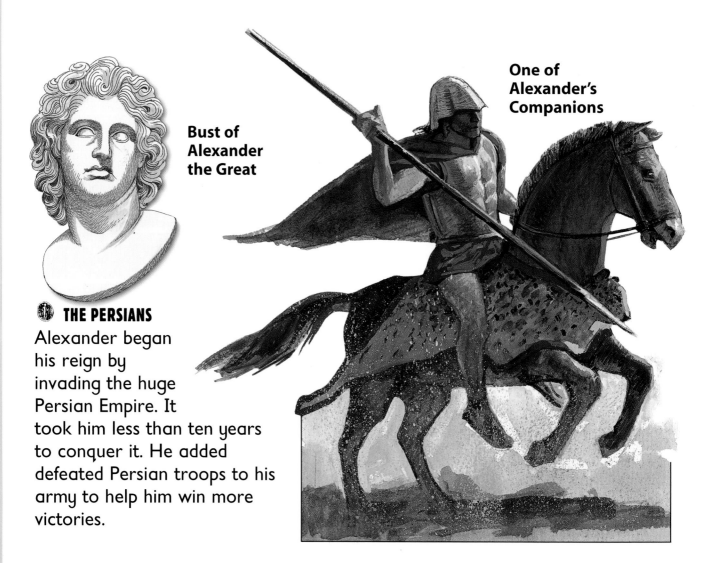

Bust of Alexander the Great

One of Alexander's Companions

THE PERSIANS

Alexander began his reign by invading the huge Persian Empire. It took him less than ten years to conquer it. He added defeated Persian troops to his army to help him win more victories.

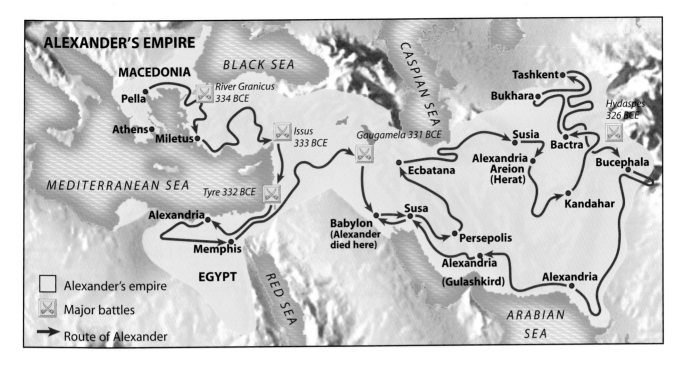

ALEXANDER'S EMPIRE

MACEDONIA
Pella
Athens
Miletus
BLACK SEA
River Granicus 334 BCE
Issus 333 BCE
Tyre 332 BCE
Gaugamela 331 BCE
CASPIAN SEA
Ecbatana
Babylon (Alexander died here)
Susa
Persepolis
Alexandria (Gulashkird)
Susia
Alexandria Areion (Herat)
Bactra
Kandahar
Tashkent
Bukhara
Hydaspes 326 BCE
Bucephala
Alexandria
Alexandria
Memphis
EGYPT
MEDITERRANEAN SEA
RED SEA
ARABIAN SEA

☐ Alexander's empire
⚔ Major battles
→ Route of Alexander

END OF THE CAMPAIGN

Alexander's campaign got as far as India and he fought a battle at Hydaspes. But his troops were exhausted and refused to go any further. Alexander was forced to return to Persia.

ELEPHANTS

In India, Alexander saw elephants being used in the army and he began to use them too. The Greeks took many elephants from India back to Greece.

Greek war elephant ready for battle

Alexander
• *Alexander was only twenty years old when he took over power.*

• *He was brave but could also be very cruel and ruthless.*

• *He was a brilliant speaker, inspiring his troops to fight hard in battle.*

• *He died of a fever in Babylon in 323 BCE.*

GLOSSARY

First century BCE = 1–99 BCE
Second century BCE = 100–199 BCE
Third century BCE = 200–299 BCE
Fourth century BCE = 300–399 BCE
Fifth century BCE = 400–499 BCE
Sixth century BCE = 500–599 BCE
Seventh century BCE = 600–699 BCE

A date with "BCE" after it means "before the Common Era" (or "before the birth of Christ", also written as "BC"). A date with "CE" before it means "Common Era" (or "after the birth of Christ", also written as "AD").

Piper playing the auloi

Allies
Countries that support each other.

Blockade
To use ships to block off an enemy's port.

Campaign
The period of time when an army is fighting an enemy.

Cavalry
Soldiers who fight on horseback.

Citizen
A free man within a city-state. He was expected to fight if there was a war.

City-state
A community of people in and around a city or town.

Conquer
To defeat and take over (for example an army or a country).

Helots
People captured by the Spartans, who were treated like slaves. They were forced to work on the Spartans' farms.

Hoplite
Greek foot soldier with lots of weapons.

Hypaspist
Macedonian soldier who had fewer weapons than a hoplite. He fought between the cavalry and the phalangites.

Infantry
Soldiers who fight on foot.

Javelin
A spear mainly used for throwing at the enemy.

Marine
Soldier who works from a ship.

Neutral country
A country that decides not to join in a war.

Peltast
Soldier from Thrace.

Bust of Pericles

PEPIKΛHΣ

Persians
A people from Persia (now called Iran).

Phalangite
Macedonian soldier who wore little armour but was armed with a long spear (*sarissa*) and fought within a phalanx.

Phalanx
Tightly packed formation of infantrymen armed with spears. A phalanx from a Greek city-state was made up of hoplites. A Macedonian phalanx was made up of phalangites. A phalanx was from eight to sixteen rows deep. The Thebans sometimes made a phalanx that was fifty rows deep.

Philosopher
A person who studies human existence, knowledge and behaviour.

Ram
To crash into something to cause damage.

Ruthless
Someone who does everything necessary to get what he wants, however this may affect other people. Shows no kindness.

Seafaring people
A people who are good sailors, and use the sea to live and work.

Sinew
The body tissue that attaches a muscle to the bone.

Skirmishing
Form of fighting where lightly armed soldiers fight in the open.

Surgeon
A doctor who does operations.

Symbol
Something that represents (stands for) something else.

Theban
Someone from the city of Thebes.

Wisdom
The knowledge you get from things you have learned, common sense and experience.

Siege tower

INDEX